THE OLD STORY

POEMS
BY
IAN WISEMAN

Pottersfield Press
Lawrencetown Beach, Nova Scotia, Canada

Canadian Cataloguing in Publication Data
Wiseman, Ian
    The old story
Poems
ISBN 1-895900-42-5
I. Title
PS8595.I816044 2001   C811'.54   C2001-900029-4
PR9199.3.W544044 2001

Pottersfield Press gratefully acknowledges the ongoing support of the Nova Scotia Department of Tourism and Culture, Cultural Affairs Division, as well as The Canada Council for the Arts. We acknowledge the financial support of the Government of Canada through the Book Publishing Industry Development Program for our publishing activities.

Cover illustration:
Mrs. Captain B. at home in Wesleyville by David Blackwood. Used with permission of the artist.

Printed in Canada

Pottersfield Press
83 Leslie Road
East Lawrencetown
Nova Scotia, Canada, B2Z 1P8
Website: www.pottersfieldpress.com
To order, telephone toll free 1-800-NIMBUS9 (1-800-646-2879)

THE CANADA COUNCIL FOR THE ARTS SINCE 1957 | LE CONSEIL DES ARTS DU CANADA DEPUIS 1957   **NOVA SCOTIA** Tourism and Culture   Canada

For Evelyn and Nancy

Contents

Acknowledgements

The inspiration for this book comes from the Old Testament, one of the finest collections of stories I have read. The settings and details come from my own life, performed on a much less heroic scale. Real people are here, some with their own names, some with stage names, mingling with composites, elements of one personality grafted onto another, montages, the usual stew.

In an autobiographical sense, there's a gap in my writing, roughly between 1976 and 1983. During those years I lived mainly in Toronto but also in Ottawa and Halifax, worked as a TV producer, a publisher and a professor. I had a brief marriage, good friends, and many travels. The few good poems about those years (and they are very few) don't fit well into my narrative. Sorry about that.

Thanks, as always, to my parents for their help with the details of the bay poems, and to Jim Brokenshire for his help with the city poems. Thanks to my wife, Nancy Robb, the best copy editor and proofreader I know. Thanks to my publisher, Lesley Choyce, for making me feel good about the good poems and making me feel embarrassed (without meaning to) about the bad ones. Thanks to Peggy Amirault for making the text look beautiful. A special thanks to David Blackwood for making the cover look beautiful.

In the beginning

sky a perfect curve
the same shape as the silent earth
fitting every corner
or maybe there are no corners
a perfect dome
covering a perfect disc

nocturnal moon, slow-motion
in its fixed arc, and above
infinite mathematics
pinpricks scratching the blackness
blurry as I rub my welling eyes
unknowable as any heaven

Open boat I

The rain brings misery —
my coat now like the dog's,
heavy and wet,

my sandwich soft and shapeless.
Pacing the planking, edgy,
the dog is agitated,

stepping over a rolling funnel,
avoiding the engine, the gunwales,
anything that could be a crab

or a hook or a living fish.
I have this familiar feeling
we're a chorus in an old blues,

everybody knows it,
prehistoric, biblical,
paying for the sins of the world.

Full disclosure

The doctors tell Mrs. Gallagher
she is sick.
Full disclosure, they call it.

Now she's very sick
distrusting the medicine
reading about side effects

attending a support group
hearing stories of distress.
The only peace she knows

comes from her own prayers
those of her sisters
and those of her minister.

The doctors explain to her
the random kiss of sickness
the maddening sameness of science

that her mind is part of her body
but she, or so it seems to me,
doesn't believe them yet.

Life is hard and dear

The rogue fir, taller than a Christmas tree,
is growing from a crack in the cliff —
a novel place to live.

Do rains spill food down the sloping ledge?
Do seagulls leave manure?
Are there nutrients in the rock?

It looks robust enough
although, if these roots continue to thicken,
rock and tree will soon be ocean,

another page of cliff open to be read.
Life is hard and dear, Granddad says,
and it's the hardness that makes it dear.

Colin

He stands on his stage head
a light shudder, a flutter
of shoulder blades, taking flight.

Closing the rickety door
he turns to face the open water
and observes the fog bank

idling just outside the cape
and then the high cirrus
red from the receding sun.

His nets are folded for setting
Javex-bottle floats well sealed
tools back where they belong.

He's ready for the morning.
Wind and cloud now tell him
what he needs to know.

The road to Salt Cove Brook

What crow shat you, flying?
If I wasn't afraid of these boys
and desperate to be elsewhere
I'd laugh at the language.

I don't ask for their company
don't wait for the others in my class
walk alone to Salt Cove Brook
two fast miles after school.

I have time to brood, to pretend.
A hulking ore truck stops for me
a high step up to the running board.
Inside, a coarse-speaking driver

the father of a classmate
badly shaven, smoking an Export A
also a malodor of armpits
and once the racy smell of rum.

Pride

Don't show off   my mother warns me.
Don't put on airs.

When I am seven   my father is named
manager of the mine

the only enterprise   except for fishing
on this stretch of coast.

He listens to Chopin.   My mother
is reading Steinbeck.

There's no real reason   to put on airs —
everybody knows.

She will be unable   to suppress this pride
already too big.

Open boat 2

Long rollers   and high as houses.
Colin   inclines his grizzled head
leaning   toward the unseen lighthouse

finding the source   of the moaning horn.
What learning, instinct   tells him where?
Sound surrounds us   like the shouldering fog

but I have faith   he can guide us home.
A life-worn face   weathered by the bay
by tragedies.   I know his grandchild

a girl in my class   becoming
a woman   faster than the others.
In a different life   I might be one

of his tragedies   but I won't match
his knowledge of foghorns.   Colin looks
past his shoulder   a moving mountain

cold, the color of slate   above us
now beneath us   keeping his bearings
an unshakable compass   in his head.

Speaking with the dead

Hiram's family is a strange one —
they speak with the dead,
not vague thought-prayers,
but out-loud conversation.

Hiram once told me
he had spoken with his granddad,
lost in rough weather in '56
during the lobster season.

His granddad asked him
Why do you bother me?
God no longer loves you.
Soon you'll be sleeping here, too.

They buried Hiram later,
a boy who lived by the Atlantic
and never learned to swim.
Maybe they still speak with him.

The wobble

Pedalling downhill, holding on tight
trying to be bigger than the turbulence
I wobble perilously on the bike.

Looking down, I can see my legs
spring legs a gleam of bluish white
pumping hard, postponing the pain.

I see the stones, bitter, unpleasant
one-inch pieces of pale granite
jagged from a crusher at the mine.

Counteracting a skid one way
I overcorrect in another
a high-speed balancing act.

Even the handlebars are vibrating
the whole enterprise atremble —
no way out except through blood.

The brook in spring

Of the feelings of spring, I like the thaw
the best — the thrill, the liberation,
the white hills spilling their contents,

the urgent charge coursing down the brook,
headlong water. In the flooding pond
the ice, rotten with wormholes and craters,

separates from the shore, the rocks.
You have to pick your path with care.
In the growing chatter, listen — squint

at the girl taking off her parka, dance
the blood in your leg muscles, know
the shocking cold is flushing to the sea.

Tidal wave

The old people still tell the story
the terrible sucking of the undertow
the bottom of the harbor dry for a moment

one time only, followed by a howling wave
driven by an earthquake offshore
destroying buildings, livestock, haystacks

— *the soldiers, their horses, the colorbearers*
all drowned — and now peaceful again
as the currents disperse the wreckage.

Mortality

Joe's dad has a mangled hand,
crooked, dangling, still not working,
smashed by a machine at the mine.
The months of compensation are over
and he's now on welfare,
his whole family bending under the burden.

He has doubts about his God.
God may have doubts about him, too,
looking down, seeing the self-pity,
the man feeling sorry for himself,
the certainty of mortality,
the slide back down to zero.

Night fire

A fire on a beach at night
makes me think of the Stone Age
starving faces, guttering light

also of my childhood
marshmallows, green alders
overprotective parents

and later, Blue Star beer
illicit, stolen moments
phosphorescent waves

wind fanning the fire
simmering embers exploding
shining their passion again

reborn cinders dancing
lit flinders we call *flankers*
close to my clothes, flying by.

Looking down

Bent badly, a frail bird now
his body is old, his skin loose
seventy-five or eighty
his ancestors are waiting.

He dabs his dazzled eyes
still surprisingly clear
no dryness, no red, no veins
none of those fatty deposits.

Below the pontoon plane
he sees the fields, Jones's Pond
harbor squared off by the causeway
everything flat from up here.

He sees the graveyards
he knows the significance
he knows the others must know.
Man does not live by bread alone.

Separated from the flock

As we climb the ridge at Cape St. Mary's
cold and damp
— the fog moved in overnight —

a sheep in need of shearing
stands close
huge on a small hummock

calling once
barely audible above the crashing waves
the thousands of screaming birds

the foghorn's bassy blast.
The sheep looks forlorn
like one whose twin has been killed and eaten

both taken from the flock
this one sad and lost
full of the wisdom of the world.

A Spaniard abroad

Spain is good fishermen, he tells me
better seafarers, able to come so far
across the ocean to catch our fish.

Later the sailor pushes the ball past me
and I tackle him hard, no referee to see
my cleats cracking his exposed ankle.

I enjoy his cry of fairness denied
my own fierce pride, this moral duty
tainted perhaps by old prejudice

and his visible lack of certainty
the constrained face of a traveller
strange land, strange tongue, strange customs.

The Press Club

In press clubs round the world
reporters tell the same story —
I can't tell you if it's true
or where the story started.

There were two brothers
a writer who travelled abroad
witnessed great events
met the powerful and the unlucky

the other one an editor
indoors under manmade light
sickly, dithering, ignorant
knowing commas and syntax.

One night in a jealous rage
the editor killed the writer
but the evidence was weak
and a jury set him free.

Now the editor is a writer
his home lost to lawyers
his family lost to divorce
wandering the world.

The iceberg

Compressed, blue from within,
freshwater its whole life,
this piece of glacial ice

has floated in a salty river
for a thousand miles.
A high tide one night,

maybe a chance roll,
left the great iceberg
randomly wedged

in the notch of The Narrows.
For four days and nights
the ships have been waiting

in the harbor, and outside,
for a team of engineers
to detonate their dynamite.

Neil

(in memory)

1.
His Kharman Ghia   hit a truck.
Asleep?   Awake with a blown tire?
The vice-president   doesn't know.

I know.   He spent his final night
with me and some friends   without sleep
experimenting   with street drugs.

I loved to watch him paint   eyes alert
hair in pigment.   He drew a woman
abstract   a body with no head

cruel, but no one knew.   Years later
I went to her   because I missed Neil
cruel, too   but there it is.

He stole lobsters   from a holding pen
at the Logy Bay   Marine Lab
brought them to my mother   for dinner.

These cars   are killing us.
These drugs   are killing us.
Why   is no one telling us this?

2.

Neil was energy   talking, laughing
thinking quickly   exploring the edge.
On the highway   he changed to matter

a handful of chemicals   water.
People from Gander   St. John's, elsewhere
talking in groups   walking single file

through the church door   filling the grid
of the front pews   the slow order
failing to balance   the random chaos.

The Regatta

The breathiness of a squeeze-box
wheezes through the small speakers
never intended for use outdoors.

> *Auntie Mary*
> *had a canary*
> *up the leg of her drawers . . .*

Owen has the tune
maybe he's faking the words
I can't tell from his face.

> *Our local anthem*, he says,
> *Diddly, diddly, up the pond.*

On Quidi Vidi Lake the oarsmen
six on six
mark the water in a rocking rhythm.
Not a bad day, the sky almost blue
— a few clouds sailing by —
the penitentiary, the old American base
half-sheltering us
from the unpredictable breeze.
Midsummer
and already fall is in the air.

We walk the tired midway
once grass
customers tossing balls at bottles
dimes at dishes
games run by church charities
and here's Nish Collins
who writes doggerel for *The Daily News*
darkening a card table
perched above an old typewriter
behind a handwritten sign

> *Only a quarter*
> *I'll write you a poem*
> *At least you'll have something*
> *Worthwhile to take home.*

The Grad House

(for E.D.)

Taking cough medicine for a cold —
bed rest is what I need.
I eat poorly except at my girlfriend's.

She's the only one I trust,
the one who tells me I can be a boss
at the age of 24.

She is wrong. I have talents
– analysis, writing, production —
but managing people is not among them.

One beer in me already.
It's our turn at the pool table —
I break, the striped balls open up,

and I'm so relaxed
I run the entire table.
Things coming too easily.

Levitation

On the outskirts west of the city
I watch a Caterpillar backhoe
hollow a hole for a new building

and encounter a buried boulder
half as big as the machine itself.
Always, it seems to me, these rocks

have broken free from the bedrock
— a rebellious and violent act —
and floated up through the earth.

I know it didn't happen like that.
Nature has been working a long time —
outcrop, erosion, glacier, topsoil.

At the beach, a similar illusion –
unyielding eggs, massive on the sand
maybe washed up by the ocean.

Closing time

City aglow on the horizon
upside-down bowl of diffuse yellow
light pollution.

Driving hard now
trying to make it downtown
before closing time

before my friends pour forth
the street suddenly noisy
no one ready for home.

Younger brother

So far off any schedule of prediction
I didn't see it coming —
Gerry becoming a star

a sound musician, a disturbing poet
able to sadden or brighten a room.
Yesterday he was the youngest

not the smartest, not the most handsome
not the fastest, not the strongest
only the youngest

uncertain, asking if he could join us.
Sometimes we'd let him
angled ears, hand-me-down clothes

and he would be happy
deep contentment in his face
music in his crooked grin.

'62 Plymouth Fury

(for R.O'R.)

Up through the black water
red white red   red white red
six taillights shine for a full minute
as I sit on a rock in three AM air
the problem of what to blame
power brakes   power steering
gravel road   foggy night
novice driver   bellyful of beer
through a guardrail
      off a causeway
           into the ocean.

Later, things will go wrong, electrical circuits
will fail, the lights going black
on the highway at night, or
making a jump-start
      flying at sixty
           down Signal Hill.

The front has a rumpled look
not wrinkled exactly, but not straight, either
the print of a hoof up on the roof
where my father killed the horse
a faint smell of seaweed
when the heater is on
A & W burgers
      drive-in movies
           grown-up girlfriends.

Bonaventure Avenue

Close to where I stand
the taxi brakes at the curb.
The back door opens

a muffle of voices
unfamiliar legs
white, in need of sun

long, slim muscles
seat-wrecked black skirt
caught on the fabric.

I go where
a 20-year-old goes
buffeted, tossed by lust.

The woman emerges —
a beautiful face
surrounded by a nun's habit.

Progress

The potter looks troubled. She calls the clay
leather hard — precise, poetic — not yet brittle,

losing its dampness, losing its first shine.
As she breaks the deformed pot into clay again,

no longer ceramic, I look for a long time.
Soon it will be something new, something better.

Tok, Alaska, 1976

Travelling with me for two days now
this young woman from Seattle

on holiday from a nursing school
hitching across Alaska, an adventure

tells me why she's in the North
a prostitute, following the pipeline

until some unnamed thing scared her.
The dream gone wrong. Who am I to judge?

Sadness and memory in her eyes
she looks back as we cross into Canada

and I half expect she'll turn to stone.

House party

Six beers in a paper bag
from the bartender at the Ringside.
Overpriced, greedy. What can you do?

Saturday night, summer. I'm late.
Music, an Eagles song is playing
and people are talking loudly.

A pattern is repeating itself.
I recognize this song —
I can sing the backup parts.

Someone opens the door
allowing sound and smoke to escape
and a solid block of porch light.

A man I know, unhappy, too.
I ask how the party is going.
All senders, no receivers, he says.

Lunchtime at the office

One decision leads to another.
Maybe I'm unable to make decisions,

three years' working at the same place,
a mortgage, taxes to pay, soon a car,

credit cards, a family. I'm not ready yet.
Lunchtime at the office, young and old

straining to be civil, a thin camaraderie,
playing chess badly with co-workers,

listening to the flirtations of an accountant,
now sixty. Sexual dreams never die.

My colleagues fade. I'm barely breathing,
the usual strain, the unbelievable effort

to keep up my end of a conversation,
to show some pleasure, hide the pain.

Indian summer

a leaf full and red
rasps the fall asphalt
lifts in a gust of squall

thermals off the pavement
and odd crosswinds
in this two-storey corner

keep the leaf floating
on eddies of warm air
fleeting and forever

recognizing I am young
now that I'm leaving home
released and surprised

the leaf above the roofline
a horizontal torrent
across the shingles, and over

The voice

(for J.B.)

I am overeducated, logical.
I read too much — Teilhard de Chardin,
Simone Weil. Sometimes when my mind

drifts in this direction there's a hole
in my stomach, a crossroads of nerve cells,
a pang at the point where mind meets soul.

I look for God in the wrong places;
I wait for Him to look for me.
A friend of mine, preparing for a night

of beer and laughter, standing on a hill
overlooking Conception Bay, a wind
driving grit in his face, his eyes,

hears the voice of God — the God
of the Old Testament, sender of locusts,
lightning, outbreaks of sickness, saying

he must rescue his life. I've met others
with God in their lives, relaxed and happy,
no more decisions to make. This certainty

all I ever wanted — not beer, not laughter.
I want *that* voice in *my* memory.
My friend may be surprised I recall.

I know for him the voice grows faint,
he never mentions it, but some part stays
a birdwatcher, a hermit, an ascetic.

Yuri

(in memory)

Yuri and I travel south.
I insist on cheap hotels
and he doesn't believe me when I say,

It's a wonderful world.
To cheer him up I invent a song —
We're going to the Mondial,

we're going to the Mondial,
Ar-gen-TI-na!
the G pronounced like an H.

I buy him a ticket,
the quarterfinal, Italy and Holland.
He's bored by the soccer,

awed by the mood at River Plate,
the passion of 100,000 fans.
The memory of feeling, all that's left.

Osgoode, Ontario, 1984

I have no respect for reporters.
Why are so many clerics cranky,

without cheer, biased in petty ways?
Wiseman, isn't that a Jewish name?

My wife-to-be looks me a caution.
His blessing? On the Rideau River?

We'd do better to find a magistrate
to marry us, maybe a ship's captain.

Four questions

(in memory of C.S.)

Do you believe
in God?

Yes, I think,
it's the church
I don't believe in.
Holy men
performing unholy acts.

Do you believe
in Jesus Christ?

Ambiguous, this one.
Does he mean the man?
or the son of God?

Do you believe
in the Holy Spirit?

Probably not
in the sense he means.
Spirit is hard to speak of.

Will you be responsible
for this child
and her spiritual upbringing?

Simple questions,
not easy,
each one upsetting
my careful balance.

My neighbors

are a church-going lot
the women especially
mainly talk and posturing

don't treat each other well
seem unable to forgive
pass their faults to their kids.

What they really need
is a daily decency
without reference to God.

Down by the tugboats

Judgement Day is coming.
The wino is walking too close,
matted beard, filthy pants,

raincoat buttoned to his neck
even though it's sunny enough
that I wish I had a hat.

Down by the tugboats
— my favorite place in Halifax —
the oily, doltish, ocean-going tugs,

bulbous hulls, black with black tires.
I look in his restless eyes
and he looks straight through me.

Maybe boom, boom, boom, one by one,
or maybe we'll all die at once.
I have no answer.

Space metal

Her cropped hair gives me
a clear look at her ears
metallic black earrings

buzzing with strangeness.
Space metal, she tells me
small pieces of meteorite

sculpted into tiny Buddhas.
Mostly iron, she offers
maybe magnetic in some new way

or with a new atomic number
not a whole number, foreign
like Eastern music. This woman

hears Buddhist harmonies.
Through the window I can hear
the Chebucto Head lighthouse.

What's that, Daddy?

At the Hagia Sophia
I see through her eyes
the largest painting

of Christ on the cross
I have ever seen.
At the Courtauld Institute

she's transfixed by a canvas
I count maybe ten minutes
Cain nearly naked

killing his sibling, Abel.
We read the old story
The Children's Bible.

Who would have thought
a three-year-old
could lead the way?

At Aunt Molly's funeral

What does a producer do?   Uncle Keith
trying to know me better.   I try to explain
conceptual work   assignment, direction.

So you do nothing.   Laughter in the graveyard.
His wife, Aunt Evie   stares at us sternly
not warmed by our levity   catching us out.

Erik

To connect with a teenage boy
what language
after five years of silence?

Me, worldly uncle at forty.
Him, on the tightrope
between omnipotence and tears.

I try Nintendo. Useless.
He's an accomplished master
and I've never played before.

He teaches me wall badminton
fast, reflexive
shuttlecock bouncing off the siding.

Maybe this way I tell my sister
I love her
enjoying my time with her child.

The back door, open again

Asleep at the Wheel and its sweet Texas swing
chases the winter, the classical cold
putting an end to the Russians, the Finn.

The song is behind me, the sun is outside.
Black turns to green, sticky new from the old —
what winter had frozen appears to be spared.

Nancy is spreading the topsoil, rich, dark.
This, so late, finding her passions in life —
her garden, the love of a little white dog.

The dog follows, giddy that springtime has burst,
snout in the shrubbery, enjoying herself.
One rhododendron ahead of the rest.

Enemies of promise

When he listed   the enemies of promise
the literary critic was right   early success
money   journalism, book reviewing

sexual relationships, marriage   children
teaching   politics   alcohol.
I've fallen under the sway   of every one.

Clarkes Beach

My sister did a hopeful thing
an Oklahoman thirty years

as American as her grandchildren.
Visiting home she bought some land

maybe an acre of wild grassland
on a slope descending to the sea.

Our family is scattered east and west
United States, Vancouver Island

me here to stay in Halifax
all nursing a strong agitation

we cannot or will not name
and my parents ready to leave

to be closer to the lost family.
Maybe later others will return.

Children

Still I can hear them
one girl naming Adam and Eden
the Bible says it's so

my child explaining amoebas
oceans warmed by sunbeams
fossils, monkeys, slow

when an outraged woman
the mother of the religious child
joins in, defends her home

against the encroaching world
gives a punishment in anger
banishes the wrong girl to her room.

I remember my own childhood
minister outside his tiny church
bony handshake, gravel parking lot.

I put the pattern together
but even the things that once
belonged together are coming apart.

Saving my marriage

The question that can save your marriage,
he said, *is a question you ask yourself —*

What would it be like to be married to me?
Sometimes I catch a glimpse, a tone of voice,

a helpless shrug, a rolling of my eyes.
Now that I am old, an unattractive man

(bald, thin, crooked teeth), not very nice
(intolerant, insecure, judgemental)

bad husband (lazy, silent, unromantic),
unable to solve the problems of my life.

The point of no return

I can't go back now.
The climate is too wild
the North Atlantic too cold
the work too scarce.

My cousins and friends
have made their peace
an island-bastion stance
a place where it's us and them.

They know I'm not coming back
not even to a grave.
No one would forgive my sins.
At each gate, angels with fiery swords.

Meditation

the masters
know

it's not
the amount of

clean air
you breathe in

that matters
it's the amount

of stale
you expel

The brook in winter

The sound is deep, submerged –
a dream, a mirage, a memory.

I can walk across the brook
— can't now call it *the brook* —

subterranean, near *and* far.
It's down there — I know this –

but it seems to me the only brook
is an echo inside my mind.

A new beginning?

sky still a perfect curve
cold and clear
many weak stars
pinpricks scratching the blackness
one brighter star

overpowering the light from the motel
the sound of the revellers
swelling
a perfect accompaniment
for the startled cry of a newborn

AN AFTERWORD

An afterword

I have multiple sclerosis. In the summer of 1995, a loss of energy made me retire from professional activities and begin life in a wheelchair. For a few months, I wondered what to do with my time. I wanted to paint, but I no longer had the control. I wanted to write a novel, but I no longer had the stamina. And so I began to write poems, short pieces I could compose in my head and later transfer, letter by letter, to my computer.

As I wrote, I read, 200 or 300 books of poetry and poetry criticism, most of them ordered through Frog Hollow Books in Halifax (thank you, Mary Jo and Dina). And as I read, I kept this list. I had three criteria: first, each point had to be insightful about poetry; second, it had to move me, emotionally; and third, it had to fit on one line of 12-point Helvetica on my computer screen.

I kept adding to the list until the summer of 1999, when reading became impossible. My arms no longer had the strength to hold a book, my fingers no longer had the dexterity to turn pages, and my eyes no longer had the acuity to focus from line to line. So now, here is that list, as I wrote it, with all the idiosyncrasy, the disorganization, the redundancy, and the contradiction still intact.

Ian Wiseman
March, 2001

Some elements of poetry —

1. The idea.

2. Surface narrative.

3. Universal narrative (sometimes hidden).

4. Rhythm — established meter for key lines.

5. Acceleration, deceleration.

6. Not too many stresses per line, careful with offbeats.

7. Use rhyme as rhythm: internal particularly.

8. Develop assonance, consonance, for key words.

9. Load the freight into the end of poems, stanzas, lines.

10. No clichés.

11. No ambiguity, unless deliberate or magic.

12. Magic moments (intuitive, unexplained, maybe ambiguous).

13. Images (best with people, action).

14. Or metaphor (controlled, consistent).

15. Music (meter and matching sounds, consonants or vowels).

16. Slow–fast alternation, also formal vs free.

17. Variations on a theme (or repetition of a theme).

18. Structure — beginning, middle, end.

19. No loose ends — tie everything up.

20. The voice, or voices. Establish immediately.

21. The mood. Scenes, or loaded words.

22. Tension of line (sometimes slackness).

23. Balance of stresses before and after caesuras.

24. The voice must speak to some reader.

25. "Fire, not marble." — Louise Glück

26. Give the feel, the emotion, the sensation, not the facts.

27. "To name is to destroy, to suggest is to create."
    — Stephane Mallarmé

28. No glib endings — be very careful.

29. No latinate freight-train prose — lighten up.

30. Even the first line must be designed to set up the final impact.

31. A search for answers, not a pontification of answers.

32. Complex sentences to slow and develop, simple monosyllables to pay off.

33. No narcissism, self-promotion.

34. No rationalizations, no feeling sorry for oneself.

35. No depressive poetry, period. Uplift or delete.

36. Moment of crisis — turning point in poems of tension.

37. *In medias res.* Start in the middle of things.

38. Must seem natural, spontaneous, unforced.

39. Go for brevity and breathlessness. Dump the redundant.

40. Lines leading into each other — ascend, descend, anticipate.

41. Line breaks in free verse — not on full stops.

42. "What matters in poetry is what's left out." — Ezra Pound (dump the clutter!)

43. "The secret sits in the middle." — Robert Frost (get at truth indirectly)

44. Precision of description (as in Robert Ammons's *Clarity*).

45. "A poem is a high-energy construct at all points." — Charles Olson

46. One perception must lead immediately to another. Speed the essence.

47. Avoid editorializing, giving simplistic philosophies.

48. "A rhyme must have a slight element of surprise if it is to please." — Ezra Pound

49. Some poems solid as a tree, some fluid as water pouring into a vase.

50. "The lyric mentions, the reader expands the mention." — Helen Vendler

51. Stories, yes; sex, maybe; dignity always (like Virginia Adair or Hayden Carruth).

52. Poems can have meanings and statements, but must have esthetics.

53. Witness, reconstruct, record — but also use symbols and music.

54. Underneath Seamus Heaney's poetry is "a voice of secret brooding". — Helen Vendler

55. The poet presents, rather than tells about, sensory experience.

56. Even when compressed, the writing should feel leisurely, spacious.

57. A poem is a method of distinguishing, defining, limiting. — A.R. Ammons

58. The motion of a poem must resemble the motion of reality.

59. "Verse consists of a constant and a variant." — Ezra Pound

60. "Art is an activity of the spirit." — Robert Hass

61. "The process of creation is the form of unity." — Charles Olson

62. Vary the number of beats per line, even if phrases are metronomic.

63. "Repetition brings security, variation freedom." — Robert Hass

64. Safety and magic (incantation) on one hand, freedom and movement the other.

65. Rhythm — hear it, develop it, bring it to form (a close).

66. Echo the rhythms and vowels or consonants of phrases. (Gary Snyder in Hass)

67. Events within events, as in *The Explosion* by Philip Larkin. Texture, layers.

68. Gathering momentum, the pull of long lines. *Damson* by Seamus Heaney.

69. "Don't try." — Charles Bukowski (keep it unforced)

70. Keep it sexy, sad (or funny) and simple — not "difficult".

71. Discard everything that is "good enough" — exaltation on every page.

72. No prose — every section must be poetic, have energy, esthetics.

73. Unhappiness provokes poems, being happy doesn't.

74. "Novels are about other people, poems about yourself." — Philip Larkin

75. The poet usually re-creates the familiar (as opposed to the foreign).

76. Poetry readings lead to easy rhythms, easy emotions, easy syntax.

77. "I write poems to preserve things." — Philip Larkin

78. Every poem must be its own freshly created universe.

79. Poetry is emotional in nature and theatrical in operation.

80. Should have philosophical resonance, otherwise purely egocentric.

81. A burden of understanding and feeling should force the poem into being.

82. A magical illumination of the ordinary.

83. Visions of clarity and terror.

84. Intensity and perfection matter more than scale.

85. Unhurried control and a plainness of expression.

86. Don't fear the uncommon word, try to energize the common ones.

87. Not so much what it says, as how it says.

88. Build in edges and resistances, a kind of counterpoint.

89. Rhetoric okay, but must be a song, rhythmic.

90. Messages must be clear, clean, although can be complex.

91. A subtle feeling for the measure.

92. Esthetic skills must be unobtrusive (no obvious alliterations, rhymes).

93. "The cool, precise language of passion giving rise to passion." — Stephen Dunn

94. Words pushed against their meanings, syntax against its structure.

95. Should alter a reader's inward existence, change his mind.

96. Consistency of tone within each poem.

97. The best poetry sustains, rather than diverts.

98. "To find my home in one sentence, as if hammered in metal" — Czeslaw Milosz

99. Order, rhythm, form — three words opposed to chaos and nothingness.

100. A poem must bring pleasure, not be "difficult".

101. "A poem is less an orange than a grid." — Donald Davie

102. The action over quickly, leaving reverberations for the reader.

103. Straddling words, carrying two meanings, marrying two themes.

104. "All the parts of a poem must be alive." — Ted Hughes

105. The living parts of a poem — words, images, rhythms.

106. Living words activate the five senses — click, freckled, vinegar, onion.

107. Other living words act, are muscular, like "flick" or "balance".

108. Be careful the side meanings of words don't cancel each other.

109. "A headlong, concentrated improvisation on a set theme" — Ted Hughes

110. Poetry is made from experiences that change our body, mind, spirit.

111. Writing about people — precise, idiosyncratic, descriptive flashes.

112. A whole life can be suggested by a single incident.

113. A poem should concentrate on one thing, avoid tangents.

114. Or a procession of thoughts, as a story or an argument.

115. Careful not to separate adjective and noun by line break.

116. "Poetry is closer to prayer than to prose." — Franz Kafka

117. Striving to say what can't be said.

118. "Only connect" — E.M. Forster

119. The reader must suddenly sense he is not alone.

120. Affirming the value of even the smallest thing.

121. A single line can lead us into a new meditation.

122. A good poem leads the reader into himself.

123. "Poetry is like being alive, twice." — Chinese proverb

124. Line breaks must have a textual, metrical or syntactical reason.

125. The light shining behind the poem.

126. The vision is as important as the art.

127. Composition — metric, rhyme, structure, syntax.

128. Imagination is useless unless brought to bear on reality.

129. "Poems are unified by infinite and indefinable connectives." — Hayden Carruth

130. "Transcendence — toward light and music and silence" — George Steiner

131. Try for feelings and meanings larger than those stated.

132. "Any object looked at intently enough becomes symbolic." — Theodore Roethke

133. The motive for writing a poem is its substance, what it's about.

134. Proper rhythm, as in music, sets up an anticipation of the next beat.

135. The phrasing, as in music, may ride separately from the rhythm.

136. Not a linear unrolling of printed sentences, but artful speech.

137. Meanings should echo, not just sounds.

138. The pathos and sweetness and power of plain song (no allusions).

139. Two kinds of expressiveness — sensual and conceptual.

140. Boil it all down to the nub.

141. Poetic virtues — first, lucidity and authenticity, second, honesty and decency.

142. Final word in a line naturally emphatic.

143. Tension between the conscious and the unconscious.

144. Conclude a poem without sealing it off — leave room for the reader.

145. Throughout a poem there must be room for the reader's own thoughts.

146. "Major components of lace: air, perforations and truancy." — Osip Mandelstam

147. Don't try for "poetic" — common diction will do.

148. "A poem is finally just a natural thing." — James Laughlin

149. "Illumination of a surface, the movement of a self in the rock." — Wallace Stevens

150. "Imagination loses vitality when it fails to adhere to reality." — Wallace Stevens

151. "Poetic genius — passion is calmed, calm is passionate." — Benedetto Croce

152. Beware of preciosity and affectation.

153. A balance between imagination and reality.

154. "The very image of life expressed in its eternal truth."
— Percy Bysshe Shelley

155. The essence of the matter.

156. The seeds of knowledge, the truth of fact.

157. A group of images in harmony with each other.

158. When metaphor fails — incongruity, or artificiality.

159. Finding form in the middle of chaos.

160. The poetry of humanity is everywhere.

161. A universal poetry, of which specific poems are manifestations.

162. "The senses deform, the mind forms." — Georges Braque

163. The enchantments of intelligence

164. The drive of a poem is as important as the finish, the polish.

165. Beware the torpor of generic vocabulary — be specific.

166. "The reality of the world should not be underprized."
— Pablo Neruda

167. Cool compositions secreting bitter knowledge or lyrical joy.

168. "The harmonized background, the principle of tranquility" — Zbigniew Herbert

169. "The rule of the demon of perspective" — Zbigniew Herbert

170. Equally explicit and evocative

171. "The condition of complete simplicity, costing everything." — T.S. Eliot

172. "A momentary stay against confusion." — Robert Frost

173. "Formed from within, like a crystal." — Osip Mandelstam

174. "Or cut from without, like a stone." — Osip Mandelstam

175. Detail upon detail, a layering of intelligent observation.

176. Sometimes a leap to the moral, the mystical, the universal.

177. "Poetry is more a threshold than a path." — Seamus Heaney

178. "Reader (and writer) at the same time summoned and released." — Seamus Heaney

179. "A poem is an event, not a record of an event." — Robert Lowell

180. "A power, never explicated, well below the surface." — T.S. Eliot

181. Beyond ego, more than autobiography.

182. "Boldness in the face of the blank sheet" — Boris Pasternak

183. "A poem should be equal to, not true." — Archibald MacLeish

184. "A poem should not mean, but be." — Archibald MacLeish

185. "A thing is brought forth we didn't know was in us." — Czeslaw Milosz

186. "The spontaneous overflow of powerful feelings." — William Wordsworth

187. Passion — Oh, Johnny, we hardly knew ye.

188. Hearing audible patterns, sensing hidden ones.

189. "Man cannot understand without images."
— St. Thomas Aquinas

190. Memorizing poetry — meter is one useful tool.

191. Memorizing poetry — rhyme is a more useful tool.

192. Memorizing poetry — content is the most useful tool.

193. "The ghost of some simple meter." — T.S. Eliot (loose iambs)

194. Additional syllables loosen the iambic rhythm.

195. An anapest loosens iambic meter (Stevens technique).

196. Balance between firm iambs and the total collapse of rhythm.

197. "An absolute rhythm that corresponds to the emotion."
— Ezra Pound

198. "A deep-breathing economy and an organic unity."
— Henry James

199. The Coleridge formula — unity in variety.

200. A deep sense of things belonging together, inexplicably.

201. "Basic patterns are universal, are known without their names." — Richard Blackmur

202. "Occult resemblances in things apparently unlike." — Samuel Johnson

203. Harmony, propriety & enduring stability of semantics and sound.

204. "One must judge how far a thing needs explaining."
— William Empson

205. Obscurity is not altogether destructive.

206. The darkness in which meaning hides can be an important effect.

207. A good line supercedes all structural principles.

208. A poem has narrative aspects, emotional aspects, technical aspects.

209. The resonance of synchronous events, non-linear, organic, layered.

210. Making a whole of the complexities — physical, psychic, political.

211. Outward to the edge of the universe, inward to the loneliness of the self.

212. Analyzing the poet — his experience, his education, his imagination.

213. How the poet uses (a) the known, (b) the learned, (c) the made-up.

214. Experience is conveyed by physical fact and re-creation of emotion.

215. Education is conveyed by allusion, vocabulary, syntax.

216. Imagination is conveyed by overall concept and poetic technique.

217. Narrative elements and emotion elements survive translation.

218. Technical elements (meter, rhyme, consonance, onomatopaeia) do not.

Some elements of autobiography —

1. Grasping at images, then trying in vain to pull out the whole story.

2. "A desire to reduce the chaos of experience to a sort of order." — Graham Greene

3. Feel the real emotions again, without irony.

4. Remembered events, but with self-analysis, too.

5. Any aspects of observation, psychology, or confession.

6. Importance of context — description of places and times and conventions.

7. The travel writer's trade — sensory details.

8. Dignity. Suggest, but don't kiss and tell.

9. Repetition of a theme, just enough to show it repeats.

10. Later sections must show imprint of first sections.

11. Early dreams/fears, then how they turned out.

12. What is said must always be something the writer could know.

13. "What is alive in art is first the painter and second the picture." — Vincent van Gogh

14. The voice of the writer is the essential thing.

15. Anecdotes, fragments, glimpses — this is the true history, as lived.

16. A corollary — too neat an overall narrative rings false.

17. "The only important things in life are those you remember." — Jean Renoir

18. Self-assurance vs doubt — how to handle the narrator's truth.

19. An intemperate beats a sober omniscient narrator.

20. Strong opinions, even about another person, reveal the writer.

21. A full record of ambivalences, the love and the hate.

22. Treat fictional people as real (reader's sense of voyeurism, dignity).

23. We all invent ourselves.

24. Autobiography as a dream, unfathomable, from which one has yet to wake.

25. Autobiography — inconclusive by necessity, life not yet over.

26. "Narratives pale and shrink in the face of the disorderly life". — Janet Malcolm

27. "The writer faces not the blank page but his overfilled mind." — Janet Malcolm

28. Find a few ideas & images and arrange them so the reader wants to linger.

29. There's a danger in throwing out the wrong things.

30. Moods are temporary, attitudes permanent.

31. Special points to make story cold, hard, distant, authentic, believable.

32. Find the themes, the cracks in the golden bowl.

33. Mind and heart should speak as one.

34. Say what you have seen and mean what you say.

35. Voice must be trustworthy, clear and brave.

36. A vivid sense of mortality.

37. An account of the heart's dark, sometimes confused, transactions.

38. The secret life, more real, often denied.

39. Happiness is not birdsong and flowers, it's struggling in a storm.

40. Have no faith in any single-answer dogma.

41. No whining or complaining, and no sense that life is easy.

42. Celebrate and praise, as well as lament.

43. All poets suffer from vanity — this is essential.

44. Life as a chronic, low-grade emergency.

45. Life is hard and dear; and it is the hardness that makes it dear.

46. "A pose can be sincere." — Donald Justice (the use of attitude)

About the author

Ian Wiseman was born in Newfoundland in 1950, one year after Confederation. He grew up in St. Lawrence, a mining and fishing town, before studying literature at Memorial University of Newfoundland and Carleton University.

In 1968, while still in school, he began writing for newspapers and magazines. In 1972, he was hired as a television producer by the Canadian Broadcasting Corporation, where he would work, off and on, until 1995. He won an Anik Award for documentary production in 1975.

Between 1980 and 1995, he also taught at The University of King's College in Halifax, Nova Scotia, where he still holds the honorary title of Inglis Professor. He was a visiting fellow at City University in London, England, in 1988-89, and a Maclean Hunter Fellow at The Banff Centre for the Arts in Banff, Alberta, in 1993. He currently lives in Halifax with his wife, Nancy Robb, and their daughter, Evelyn.

Other books by Ian Wiseman:

A History of the End of the World. Morrow, New York, 1982 (with Yuri Rubinsky).

The Wankers' Guide to Canada. Bantam-Seal, Toronto, 1985 (with Ian Brown, Marc Giacomelli, Robert MacDonald and Yuri Rubinsky).

Home and Away. Pottersfield Press, Lawrencetown Beach, 1999.